WFH

Worki..g

MW00462009

A THRIVAL GUIDE
For Challenging Times
And Beyond

This resource book is designed to provide immediate support, tools and tips to manage stress, practice resilience, lead your team remotely, maintain your brand in a virtual world, stay healthy, improve sleep, enhance your parenting capacity and build new habits to sustain and thrive beyond 2020.

We provide HR Talent Solutions, Coaching, and creative eLearning, for individuals, teams and organizations globally. Let us help you THRIVE!

Linda Newlin, MCC
HR Strategic Partner
Master Certified Coach
Email: Info@WorkFromHome.Expert

WFH: Working From Home
A Thrival Guide
for Challenging Times
and Beyond

Author: Linda Newlin

Editors: Annie J. Dahlgren and Dorian Hollis

Cover Design: Cecilia Martini Muth, CC Design

eBook $2.99. ISBN: 978-0-9962065-4-9

Paperback $4.95. ISBN: 978-0-9962065-3-2

Library of Congress (pending):

Fast Read Books
3463 State Street, Suite 225, Santa Barbara CA. 93105
Office (805) 729-1663

www.WorkFromHome.Expert

BULK Quantity Discounts Available

Contact Us: Info@WorkFromHome.Expert

We provide leadership and development, talent acquisition, learning and development solutions, tools and coaching support to individuals, teams and organizations globally.

The world of business is experiencing a massive global experiment in Working From Home.

Even though some companies have had upwards of 40% of their workforce working virtually in the last decade, the debate continues around efficiency and effectiveness.

We are now in an instantaneous experiment as nearly a billion people are having to work from home during the 2020 global pandemic.

With any sudden change, it can bring great stress and uncertainty. It also brings tremendous opportunity.

Companies can choose to stand in the doorway and look out into the future of what might be possible if they shed the old bricks and mortar mentality to explore and reconfigure how to best work and grow going forward from here. One of the gifts of the internet is the ability for more people to be productive contributors globally from virtual remote work locations.

What will you create?

Our organization is here to support individuals, teams and companies to set up virtual coaching, gatherings and processes to navigate this unprecedented time of sudden change in our workplace biography globally.

short and on point

Dear Reader:

It's March 2020 and as a business consultant, master certified coach and HR Strategic Partner, mother and friend, I want to do my part to help alleviate the suffering of as many people as I can right now.

As a writer, this is one way that I can share resources and tools with as many people through digital book distribution and also channel my own desire to help in a time when I can't meet my clients or their teams in person anywhere in this world right now.

It is my hope that this **Thrival Guide** will provide you valuable resources, practices, tools and support to navigate this reality of *Working From Home,* whether temporarily or permanently.

I believe that the skills you learn and practice, will support you in all areas of your life as you move beyond this time. These tools will enable you to be a better human, parent, employee or leader in your organization and community now and into the future. That is my vision filled with hope and possibility!

Your presence, leadership and self-care are key to it all.

Be Well and Thrive,

Linda

Working from home used to be perceived as an ideal option for some people. It was sometimes seen as a luxury and something that many people longed for.

The advantages and disadvantages of people working from home are much debated in human resource departments, board rooms and small businesses.

Over the past three decades, organizations have experimented with allowing various job functions such as sales, IT, research and HR support, be performed from home. More and more industries move toward larger percentages of their workforce operating remotely where possible, though the effectiveness of the practice is still debated.

Employees who enjoy working from home typically report loving no commute, flexibility to work around family demands, opportunity to eat healthier and exercise more regularly, practice self-care and increased efficiency and productivity as a result of fewer interruptions. Working in slippers was also noted.

Those who don't particularly like working from home list reasons such as isolation, difficulty staying focused, loss of social connection, and home environment distractions such as children's needs or proximity to the refrigerator.

We're facing unprecedented times in our world. An estimated one billion people are now working from home and many will be there into the unforeseeable future.

Much of the world is experiencing "shelter-in" situations and unable to enjoy life as they knew it. Employees are trying to maintain business as usual when all aspects of life are anything but usual.

People are experiencing stress that they've likely ever known before. To some it feels like living in a war zone, as isolation, fear about the future, financial pressures, health issues, life and death situations, grief and loss, confusion, denial and panic are all happening within or around us.

Many people are experiencing a rollercoaster effect of feeling calm, centered and grounded one minute and filled with despair and apocalyptic thinking the next.

First and foremost, there is the unknown factor. Dealing with the unknown is not easy for most people, especially those who like to have a plan. Planners are likely to experience additional stress given the uncertainties and unknowns about what the future holds.

Because this exact experience is unprecedented for all of us, no one readily has the answers or the road map to easily navigate it.

This book will help the leaders in your organization, as well as you, individually, to focus on ways to support everyone during this time of great challenge and a future with so many unknowns.

These resources, life skills and leadership tools will also further the development of critical capacities your organization will need to survive and thrive after 2020.

A THRIVAL GUIDE is designed to give game-changing, quick and useful tools, tips and practices to help you build resilience in yourself and your team, to work and lead most efficiently and effectively from home. It also includes life changing resources and skills for parents.

It's my hope that you will each find high impact lasting results in these scientifically-proven tips and resources to help support you and your unique situation during this difficult time, and beyond.

I can imagine you are doing the best you can thus far. It doesn't seem possible what is happening all around the world right now.

I know we all wish it weren't so.

Chapters

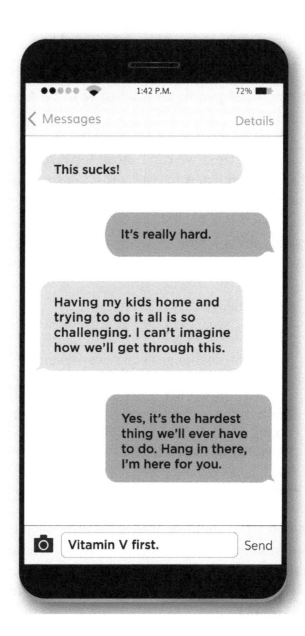

THE POWER OF VALIDATION

It's what I call **Vitamin V**.

Right now what people need most is to be heard and VALIDATED.

When we feel stress we can't move forward, unless we take the time to listen to each other and validate how hard things are.

Something shifts inside us when we follow this simple process:

1. Acknowledge this sucks
2. Acknowledge this is hard
3. Name the challenges you're experiencing
4. Identify the support you want/need?
5. Look for opportunities this situation could bring about. What good might come from this challenging situation?

It's important to do steps 1-4, prior to step 5, as this allows us to move out of our "hijacked" place of high stress and fight, flight or freeze to come back into the present moment and resource ourselves. When people are stuck, it's often because they haven't allowed themselves to name the first two steps before trying to jump to number five.

VITAMIN V

1000 MG

IMMUNE SUPPORT
Validation Boosts Positivity* and Improved Sleep

Daily Dosage Recommended

Name 3 Things You Did Well Today
write them down or share orally with others

Best taken during team meetings or one-on-ones
Can also be given at meals as a family
Or before bed

*May provide an antidote for disengagement and low
morale in teams

VALIDATE SELF and OTHERS
Text Messages Work Well for Immediate Impact

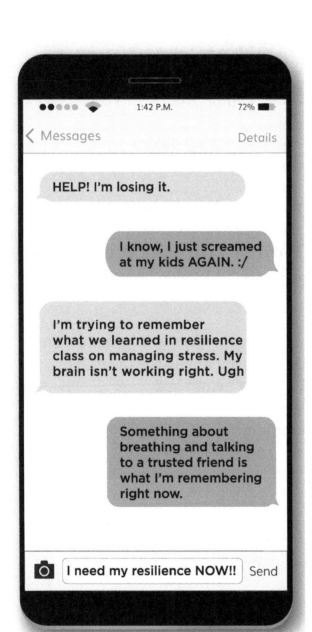

Resilience Practices
Right Now!

BEING CENTERED VS. STRESSED

When we are stressed, we react with our fight, flight, or freeze survival instincts. This natural biological operating system serves a very important function when we're in situations where we need to act and respond quickly in order to survive or save another person.

Neuroscience has helped us to identify this part of our brain which is called the amygdala, a tiny organ that is also called our reptilian or primitive brain.

The amygdala responds in 0.7 seconds when it perceives real or imagined threats by flooding our bodies with stress hormones (adrenaline and cortisol) that allow us to respond in an instant or lift a car off a child. This is what creates the fight, flight, or freeze response. Every brain has one and every person has survival instincts that cause these reactive behaviors.

When we are in a stress reaction, we do not operate at our best. I refer to it as being "knocked off center." Our thinking brain has gone off-line and our emotional brain has taken over.

It is difficult to focus and be present when stress reactions are present, and it happens to everyone.

I think the term "amygdala hijacking" is perfect because when we're in fight, flight or freeze mode, we are going somewhere we don't want to go, and it happens so fast, we can't stop it.

It's as if someone else has control over our body. We often say and do things we later regret, and/or we withdraw, withhold or shut down and disconnect from the ones we love most.

When our bodies are flooded with stress hormones, the increased cortisol levels actually diminish our oxytocin, which is the hormone that love induces and makes us feel connected.

Therefore, when we're under continued stress, we are likely to act off-center, feel disconnected and have a reduced functioning of our immune system.

In these times especially, we must take great care of ourselves and employ all of the resiliency practices we can in order to stay centered and present. (Those around us are likely to be more reactive now too!).

It's important to have compassion for ourselves and each other as we all find our inner resources and the way back to center.

Remember the last time you were "hijacked"

Did you experience fight, flight or freeze?

Most importantly, what did you do to get "back to center?"

Some Resiliency Practices Include:

- Take a break/remove myself from the situation
- Go for a walk
- Slow down, count to 10 and breathe
- Get out in nature
- Talk to a friend or loved one that I trust
- Have a good cry (this lowers cortisol levels)
- Scream, yell or howl at the moon
- Write an anger letter/email (do not send - burn)
- Exercise/sports/fishing/sailing
- Hit a punching bag
- Vent to someone who listens and doesn't judge
- Breathe
- Sleep on it
- Meditate/pray/be grateful (Vitamin G)
- Sing or play an instrument/listen to music
- Dance/yoga/massage
- Hot bath/shower/sauna
- Pet my animals
- Paint/create art/make something
- Read/write/journal
- Clean/organize/bake/cook/garden
- Play games
- Laugh/share jokes/watch comedy
- Hugs and physical touch
- Turn off devices and TV/do a media fast
- Give back to someone in need/help others

This is only a partial list of common resiliency practices. You likely have your favorites and "go to" activities depending upon the circumstances and timing of the hijacking you're experiencing.

Please notice that **Breathing** is mentioned twice. **This is because one of the fastest ways back to center is to BREATHE.**

SOME BREATHING TECHNIQUES

2X Breathing
Inhale for 2 long counts, exhale for 4 counts
Inhale for 3, exhale for 6
Inhale for 4, exhale for 8

Circular Breathing

Block right nostril with right thumb inhale through left
Hold breath at the top of the inhale
Block left nostril with right hand ring finger
Exhale through right nostril
Inhale through right nostril
Hold breath at the top of the inhale
Block right nostril
Exhale through left nostril, Inhale through left nostril
Block left nostril exhale through right nostril
Repeat several times

Physiologically, our bodies can calm the parasympathetic nervous system with our breath.

Circular Breathing also helps to integrate the left and right brain hemispheres. It's an excellent way to start any meditation practice. I use it when a specific project requires my full brain capacity!

Another breathing technique that is incredibly effective in stress management and sustainable behavior change is from the world-renowned Heart Math Organization.

Heart Math Quick Coherence Technique

Sit and breathe
You can do this with eyes open or closed
Bring attention to your heart
Take slow easy refreshing breaths in and out
Imagine your breath is coming in and out of your heart
See it coming in and swirling in to your heart and out
Think of someone you love or remember a time you felt
joy and relive the memory or the emotions of love
Continue breathing in and out of your heart space as
you experience these memories and feelings
Open your eyes and try to hold on to the feeling state
This creates quick heart resonance and deep presence.

What would be possible if you could go through your day from this inner state?

An old Aikido master's student said to him, "Oh master, you never get knocked off center." The master said, "Oh yes I do, I just know how to get back to center more quickly."

We all get knocked off and have reactive responses. How we practice getting back to center is what matters.

It's helpful to create your home and working environment with resiliency built into your space whenever possible. For instance, bringing nature inside can have a positive effect while working from home. The use of plants, flowers or pictures of your favorite natural setting is helpful if you can't sit by windows with lovely views.

Playing your favorite music or allowing breaks to relax and breathe during your day will help keep you centered and productive.

The more resilience you practice, the less likely you are to be triggered by the stress, other people, and circumstances.

Teach your loved ones and team members about resiliency. Better yet - do some practices together!

Resiliency is our capacity to recover quickly from difficulties and stress.

The more resilient you are, the more FREEDOM you have to CHOOSE how you want to respond in any given moment.

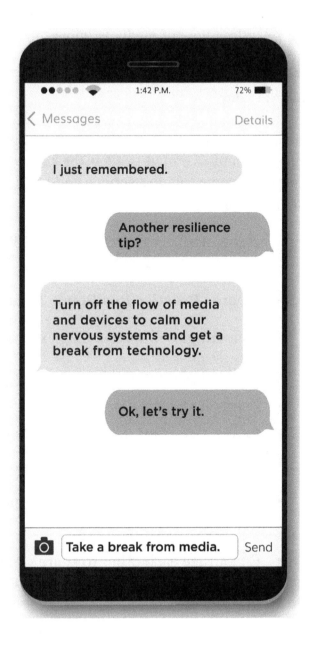

The relentless flow of media is known to cause stress and trauma reactions in people. It's a good experiment to escape from device and media input for a while each and every day.

Encourage your teams and friends/family to take breaks from media input to allow their sensory input to experience some calming periods and FOCUS on more positive things.

Implementing Resiliency Practices Is Key Right Now

Ways Teams Practice Resilience Together

Begin meetings with presencing exercises:

- Turn off phones and focus
- Everyone take 3-5 deep breaths
- Become present
- Each person share how they feel
- Vitamin V—Validate how challenging this is
- Encourage each other to share what resiliency practices they're using right now to cope.

Teams are much more efficient and creative when they're FOCUSED and PRESENT.

As work configurations continue to evolve, long after the global pandemic has passed, skills learned here can continue to be cultivated into the future.

Practice is what gets you to where you want to be.

This guide book is filled with practices to help you thrive and get to where you need to go in your organization, your family and in our world.

As Marshall Goldsmith's book reminds us.

"What got you here,
Won't get you there."

VITAMIN G

1000 MG

BRAIN and HEART SUPPORT
Calms Nervous System

Daily Dosage Recommended

Name 3 Things You Are **Grateful** for

write gratitude's down or share orally with others

Best taken during team meetings or one-on-ones
Can also be done at meals as a family
Or before bed

May provide an antidote for stress and heartache*

Gratitude may positively impact our body's chemistry
and bring immune boosting effects.

*According to recent neuroscience discoveries

Research also shows it helps psychologically
and can improve sleep when practiced often

Leading from Home

What Your Team Needs Now

And in the Future

Be Present
and Centered

~

Listen
and Support

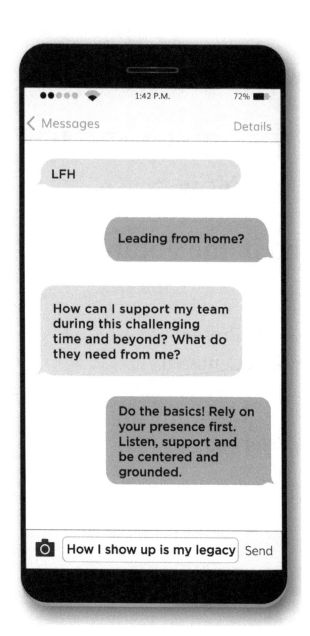

LFH

Leading from home?

How can I support my team during this challenging time and beyond? What do they need from me?

Do the basics! Rely on your presence first. Listen, support and be centered and grounded.

How I show up is my legacy   Send

Think about the worst boss you've ever worked for.

They likely had some of the following characteristics/behaviors: unpredictable, volatile, highly stressed, disorganized, uninspiring, blamed others, lacked empathy, took all the credit, controlling, unsupportive, critical, demeaning, all about the work, impersonal, lacking transparency, refusing recognition of others' contributions, talked more than listened, had erratic moods, lacked integrity, exhibited poor communication, and other negative qualities not listed.

Now think of the best boss you've worked for.

Their qualities/behaviors may have included: calm, composed under pressure, listened well, compassionate and understanding, gave positive feedback, supportive of development and career aspirations, was human and kind, courageous, decisive, humble, passionate, had keen instincts, open minded, communicated clearly, was emotionally intelligent, managed stress well, showed trust, was strong, had our backs, able to keep the team moving forward in difficult times, acted in the best interest of the team.

Which of these are you?

You are now leading and working in uncertain times. You must be your best self as much as possible.

In an ideal world, how would you like to show up for your team and your organization?

EMOTIONAL INTELLIGENCE

Research has determined that your emotional intelligence EI is a stronger determining factor in your leadership success than your intellectual IQ.

These five EI capacities are helpful to reference as you refine and develop your ability to lead, support and navigate what is happening now and in the future:

1. **Intrapersonal** – How well do you know yourself? Do you own your reactions? Can you name your inner state and emotions?
2. **Interpersonal** – What is your level of empathy? How comfortable are you with others' emotions? Do you build trust and connection?
3. **Adaptability** – What is your comfort level with change, shifting gears, dealing with unknowns?
4. **Stress Management** – Ability to get back to center after being hijacked. Resilience practices to help keep you centered more readily.
5. **General Mood** – Are you generally positive and upbeat? Research shows that productivity may increase by 27-30% when the boss is happy.

Your legacy and brand as a leader are on the line. You have a great opportunity to make a real difference in many tangible ways. Your mindset and mood are key. What lights you up and makes you happy?

If you can be present, centered and authentic you will provide a solid ground for your team to stand on. Getting back to the "High Impact Basics" is what is needed most.

Listening is first and foremost.

Let them have time to connect with each other and with you about what is hard about this time. Let them share their challenges at the moment. (Interpersonal EI)

Practice Validation - fill them with Vitamin V. When people are listened to, they feel truly heard and seen. Once people "empty out" they can shift and move beyond the stress and begin to regulate their nervous system to be more present and focused on the work at hand.

No one has navigated this unprecedented reality before. Including YOU! Take it one day at a time and use your head and your heart.

GET RESOURCED WITHIN YOURSELF FIRST

Your team needs you to model what they need.

Walk Your Talk – Be Real and Lead Well

1. Validate yourself

2. Acknowledge for yourself that this is hard

3. Name your own challenges

4. Identify the opportunities that are here now

You may also be feeling more alone in your leadership role, working from home. Be sure to find connections where you can be heard, so you can "empty out" too. You cannot underestimate the power of listening and being listened to. Ask for the support you need and want.

Let me say it again, **you cannot underestimate the power of listening**.

True listening is not about fixing, it's about being curious about what someone is experiencing and allowing them to be heard. Being seen and heard is one of our primary needs, and during stressful situations, we need it even more. Unexpected change can create surprising levels of stress.

What Your Team Likely Needs from YOU

LISTEN and SUPPORT them while they find the inner resources to navigate their stress and current realities at home. Keep connected to individuals and the team. Facilitate cohesion and schedule regular video meetings. You might host lunch and learn sessions or social events like tea time or resilience practice time. Or just zoom lunches to socialize together.

Creative solutions may be required as you help your team with technical issues as they set up home "offices."

Many will need support and understanding as they deal with new family demands (e.g., home schooling kids) while trying to maintain productive work lives.

Have meetings that foster community, connection and empathy for their circumstances, during these challenging times.

Some questions you might ask the team:

How do you want to navigate this time together as a team?

What resources and support can I provide?

What obstacles might get in the way of your being fully present during team calls/video meetings?

Asking powerful questions and listening is a coaching approach to leading that allows for more trust, connection and development.

People who listen with curiosity and an intention to learn something they don't know are much more effective in building relationships that engage and retain talent.

This is using more of a coaching approach to leading your team. Asking more and listening vs. telling and directing. How many people do you know (yourself included) like to be told what to do?

The more we can find ways to incorporate powerful questions and presence-based listening, the more trust and connection we will build with the people we lead and live with. This is a legacy you can be proud of.

Managing Your Brand Virtually

WARNING:

Your Strengths Under Stress

Can Derail You

People will judge you by your actions,
not your intentions.

Funny how we want people to judge us
by our intentions.

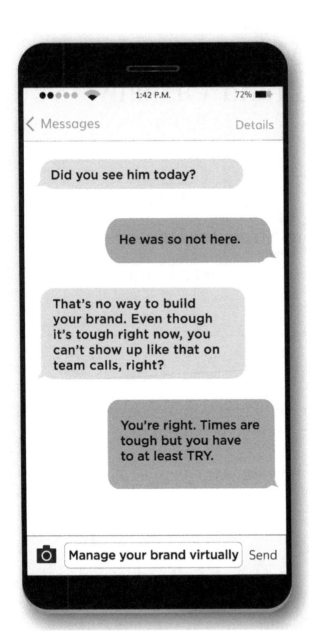

Managing and building your brand takes focus, especially in times of great stress and uncertainty. Your brand/reputation is built upon your strengths and how you show up in your life and career.

Now is the time to use your strengths effectively to serve your team, family and community well. When we're stressed, overused strengths have the potential to become career derailers.

For example: If you're highly passionate about your work, you might find yourself being perceived as too intense or moody.

If you're typically very perceptive and insightful, you may become cynical, negative, distrustful or fault finding.

If you're typically confident and assertive, you may become arrogant and entitled.

If you're typically detailed and conscientious, you may become perfectionistic and nit-picky.

If you're normally very flexible and adaptable, you may become highly distracted and unable to focus.

If you're typically strategic, you may find yourself wanting to get into the weeds and details to feel safe.

<u>You are the Decisive Element</u>

"I have come to the frightening conclusion that I am the decisive element.

It is my personal approach that creates the climate.

It is my daily mood that makes the weather.

I possess tremendous power to make life miserable or joyous.

I can be a tool of torture or an instrument of inspiration.

I can humiliate or humor, hurt or heal.

In all situations, it is my response that decides whether a crisis is escalated or de-escalated, and a person humanized or de-humanized.

If we treat people as they are, we make them worse.

If we treat people as they ought to be, we help them become what they are capable of becoming."

- *Goethe*

Emotional intelligence and intrapersonal self-awareness will always be critical to your success.

Take care to notice and recognize if you're in a negative mindset, or more volatile or reactionary than usual. You can check in with others on the team and ask for feedback if you're unsure of how you're showing up on video calls, phone calls and virtual events.

Your reputation is built on how you use your strengths for good. You are the decisive element.

Other things that are important to keep in mind as you work from home are:

- Maintain professional dress while on video calls (unless it's pajama or dress up day for fun)
- Control the sounds of pets and others sharing your space when possible.
- Mute your computer sound when you aren't speaking.

Be mindful of your stress levels and practice SELF CARE and resilience to sustain and build your brand.

What SELF CARE practices do you engage in?

SELF CARE
Game Changing Habits

Scientifically Proven to
Make You Better
at Work and Life

We need to be good at life and work. Period.

What are the practices and behaviors you engage in that make you good at life?

For me, it's following a scientifically proven and personally tested list of behaviors that have been game changers for me as a business owner, a coach, board member, a single parent and a human being.

Like any tools, these aren't useful if they're not used on a regular basis. The list below is not exhaustive, but includes some of the things that support our body's physiology to be more resourced, focused and healthy, so that we can be present and navigate the demands of day to day living.

A strengthened immune system is another key outcome of these SELF-CARE practices:

- Meditating
- Exercising
- Healthy Eating
- Limiting Sugar, Wheat, Alcohol
- Visioning Positive Outcomes
- Disconnecting from Technology
- Quality Sleeping

MEDITATION

Scientists have been studying the long-term effects of meditation for many years, and have found that people who meditate have different experiences of reactivity than people who don't. Meditation has been found to decrease systemic inflammation while increasing attention spans and improving the mental factors that control how a person behaves while trying to achieve a goal.

Meditation actually changes the way we think, work and sleep which ultimately improves our physical health.

Some studies show that meditators make more confident and better decisions, problem-solve more creatively and intuitively, and thus likely more innovative.

Meditation increases consciousness and your ability to hold multiple things at one time. This means people can be presenting at a board meeting and also be aware of the energy and emotional state of the room.

What is your current capacity to detect subtleties and themes going on around you? How is your intuitive intelligence?

Harvard Medical School professor, Srin Pillay, suggests that we need to schedule time for the brain to *unfocus* every day so that we can better focus when needed.

I heard Emily Fletcher, Ziva Founder in NYC, and author of **Stress Less, Accomplish More** say, "we don't meditate to get good at meditation, we meditate to get good at life." I encourage you to meditate daily.

EXERCISE

There is no need to explain why exercise is a game changer. Some of the outcomes you can expect are:

- Better sleep
- More focused attention/concentration
- Healthier immune system
- Higher self-esteem
- More confidence
- Better balance
- Lowered blood pressure
- Lower risk of diabetes and obesity
- Less amygdala hijackings
- Heightened feeling of being centered
- Better look and feel
- Increased executive presence
- Increased positive self esteem

You are what you eat and your brain and body work on what fuel you put in it.

You only get one body for this lifetime.

What are you feeding your one precious body suit?

The first important fuel your body needs is WATER.

Dehydration affects your brain and body and your body becomes easily dehydrated after six to eight hours.

Dehydration impacts your ability to focus, be productive and stay healthy. If you drink twenty ounces of water upon waking, you may not need caffeine.

THE BODY PREFERS HIGH OCTANE FUEL:

Vegetables

Protein

Healthy Fats

Fruit

The Body Does NOT Operate Well When We Consume:

Sugar - causes inflammation, hot flashes, reduced immune function, mood swings and is known to feed cancer cells

Wheat - can cause brain fog, skin issues, unexplained weight gain, inflammation and sluggishness

Alcohol - reduces your judgement, raises blood sugar levels, can trigger amygdala hijackings and career derailing behaviors, reduces reflexes and balance

Drugs - no need to say more

THE POWER OF VISIONING

High performing sports athletes have used visioning for decades now. Science has shown that you can imagine practicing and the body doesn't know the difference between doing it and envisioning it.

Einstein said, "Your imagination is a preview of life's coming attractions." Therefore, building in a daily practice of visualizing how you want to be throughout your day and imagining what you want to accomplish can be a very useful tool.

Before getting out of bed in the morning, envision yourself performing at your highest ability.

Imagining yourself making choices about your SELF CARE immediately upon waking will increase the likelihood that you will actually meditate, exercise, eat healthfully, etc. throughout your day. It's a form of rehearsing. This may prove to be one of your key game changers.

Helping your team take a moment to visualize how they want their work life to unfold in their current realities would be a very useful experiment.

If you have children at home from school right now, envision how you want to navigate the additional stressors that can arise and rehearse how you want to BE with them.

This is putting our brains to good use first thing upon waking!

You can also use this tool right before you have a difficult meeting or conversation. Visualize how you want it to go and what outcomes you desire.

This visioning practice grounds you back to WHO YOU ARE WHEN FULLY PRESENT and WHAT YOU WANT to move towards.

DISCONNECTING FROM TECHNOLOGY

There is plenty of data to support WHY to do it. Most important: when our devices are not in view, we can be more present to ourselves and others experience us as more available to them.

> One study showed a three-fold increase in the perceived amount of time spent with another person simply by having the phone completely out of view. This means when you connect with your children with no phone in sight (or heard ringing elsewhere), they perceive that you spend three times as much time with them.

The return is worth giving the phone a rest.

New brain studies are showing when focused work is interrupted, the brain can take more than 20 minutes to regain its prior level of focus.

Consider this high cost of constant interruptions by your technology right now.

Managing our attention is a "superpower for life". According to Mike Normant, author of *Coach Your Self Up*.

How can we support each other to FOCUS more?

What adjustment might you make to reduce the amount of times a day you check email?

Might you ask your team/organization to write URGENT in the subject line if a response is needed within three hours?

Could you request a text instead of an email if an urgent matter needs attention?

Might your assistant check for critical communications that require your response? (if you're lucky to have one)

QUALITY SLEEP

Regular, quality sleep is a crucial component of self-care. Getting enough high-quality sleep is easier to achieve when you are using all the tools already covered.

Sadly, many people suffer from sleep issues in our modern world today.

What is the quality of your sleep?

How are your family members and team members sleeping?

Technology may be negatively impacting their sleep.

Research shows it's best to turn all devices off, if possible, two hours prior to sleeping. It's recommended that your bedroom be a place for sleep and sex only.

This means no technology in the bedroom including TV's, tablets, computers and cell phones.

Some people use a timer to turn their Wifi routers off at night so their household has a break from the constant EMF's. *Note: It also helps to keep your teenagers from using the web late at night when they need to be sleeping or studying.

If your home office must be in the bedroom, it's best to turn all equipment off at night and cover it with a screen or drape to keep your mind off work while trying to connect and rest.

The brain remembers the last thing it did before sleep. If your children/teens studies first, then watches TV or any screen, they likely won't recall their studies as readily. They'll remember the characters from shows, or games more easily.

There is an interesting fact about the earth's energetic cycles to consider as well, as we seek to improve sleep.

Have you ever noticed if you're not in bed at 10 p.m., you experience a "second wind" and end up staying up until 1:00 or 2:00 in the morning?

Conversely, if you're up late and you're not up by 6:00 a.m., you find it hard to get up out of bed and feel sluggish until you get caffeine?

When I learned this information, I was a classic night owl. I didn't think I could change my sleep habits, nor was I sure that I wanted to.

However, when I had a child at 40, it was critical that I shift my rhythms and get more sleep. This has been a game changer for me the past 10 years. I highly recommend it.

If you are in bed with the lights out at or before 10:00 p.m., you are in sync with the earth. After 10:30, the earth moves to a LIGHT Pitta energy which is the "second wind" we experience.

After 6:00 a.m., the earth becomes Kapha, which is a heavy molasses-type energy.

When I started going to bed at or before 10:00 p.m., I would naturally wake up without an alarm clock between 4:00 and 6:00 a.m. I awakened alert and with amazing energy. After a decade I can attest to how well this method has worked not only for myself, but also for hundreds of my coaching clients and teams who have experimented with it.

We can even suffer less jet lag when traveling. This is a major game changer.

Light from outside and/or blue light emitted by tech devices is another thing that can impact sleep patterns for some. If you have sleep issues, you might benefit from darkening the room.

Happy Sleeping! ZZZZZZZzzzzzzz

Setting Up Your Home Office Space

Making the Most

of What you Have to Work With

and

Game Changing Efficiencies

Prioritizing what's most important in a home office space is fairly easy.

HIGH SPEED INTERNET CONNECTION
If you do any work via video-conference, it's critical that you have a strong/fast WiFi connection at least 50-60 Mbps speed. More is better, but not necessary to support you if you're not doing technical development from home.

Check with your internet provider to confirm that the connection they provide is capable of delivering higher speeds should you need it. You can check your current speed by searching "WiFi speed test" or call your provider.

Some companies offer their employees a home tech allowance to help cover service costs and additional equipment needs, depending upon the nature of your work requirements.

LARGER MONITOR
Working on a bigger monitor, if you have space, will ease eye strain.

STANDING DESK/COUNTER TOPS
If you have a choice about where you set up your work space, it's ideal to have the opportunity to work standing up, for some or all of your workday.

Sitting is the new smoking, so it's important to regularly stand up/move around, or work exclusively from a standing position, and/or stand during conference/zoom calls.

If you're able to work from an actual standing desk or a counter, you'll feel the benefit of increased energy, improved health and a more grounded feeling in your body.

BALANCE DISC/STABILITY WOBBLE
Standing on a balance disc while you work can help to tighten your core muscles, improve balance and keep your body fit while you work. It also gives your feet and knees a break from standing in one place too long.

EXERCISE WORK BIKE/EFFICIENCY PLUS
I recently updated my work space with an EXERWORK brand foldable indoor bike, which comes with a work table. Now, I easily incorporate at least 90 minutes of slow to moderate cycling into each day. To increase my focus and efficiency, I established a schedule whereby I read and reply to email 3 times per day from the bike. Not only do I exercise while checking email, I am able to give my full attention to my other work, during other times.

Other things that are important to keep in mind as you work from home are:

FOCUSING ATTENTION/BOUNDARIES
Managing distractions while working at home is one of the hardest things to master.

If you have kids at home, setting schedules for meals and breaks, and establishing boundaries around work time, will enable you to find and keep a rhythm. Experiment with different options—you'll find what works best.

Options to consider:

- Getting up earlier to have the focused work or quiet time before others in the house are up.
- Wearing a headset with music on so you don't hear what others in the house are doing while you have to focus on work
- Playing sound machines to block out distracting sounds from neighbors
- Posting Do Not Disturb sign during calls and conferences (and establish how/when to be interrupted for emergencies)
- Establishing a family system that works for you and your unique circumstances
- Placing large water bottle/kettle/coffee maker in your workspace to reduce distractions.

VIRTUAL MEETINGS

Continue to dress according to your company culture. It will help you maintain your professional brand and attitude.

I refer to this as the "as if" mode of working from home. I always keep a scarf and a sweater or jacket close by, for video calls. One of my clients can't work without shoes on because he feels "out of sorts" and unprofessional, while another works in sweats, with a silk scarf draped over herself during web calls!

It's also nice to have a colorful backdrop, piece of art or plant behind you when the video camera is on. Zoom and other video conference services now offer virtual backdrops. It gives people the illusion that you have an actual office space, even if you're working in a tiny corner of your flat. I've also seen nice shots of islands or the golden gate bridge. Just be mindful of what is the "cultural" and client expectations.

Key Warning: Prior to joining video conferences, be careful your surrounding appears professional and on brand. Don't allow others to see your laundry basket or bathrobe. If you must work from your bedroom, it's best not to be snuggled on the bed with pillows behind you while meeting with clients. Unless you're selling mattresses of course! ☺

WORK/LIFE BALANCE

This is another challenging aspect of WFH. Some people report working longer hours during challenging times like these, while others struggle to find enough time to manage work responsibilities while constantly met with family demands.

What can you shift to find more focused stretches of time to perform your work?

If you're working too many hours, you'll need to practice setting healthy (saying "no/not today") around your work load and prioritize tasks with something like an A-B-C system:

  A – Complete as first priority
  B – Complete by end of business day
  C – Complete as soon as you can

Communicate priorities openly and regularly, with your team and stakeholders. Open communication is key.

If you're practicing good self-care, your own focus will be increased. Remember to hydrate well, feed your body healthy fuel throughout your day and try the exercise bike-working technique. Know that eating and drinking healthfully fuels your brain to work most efficiently.

At the end of the work day, close the door and/or turn off devices, take Vitamin V, Vitamin G and sleep well.

Resourceful and Effective Parenting
Day by Day

Dear Parent:

This Chapter is about the inner work required to show up, repair and cultivate resilience in your family as well as build new capacities that will sustain you through the long days of parenting.   There are no instruction manuals designed for this work, however, I will share a few life changing tools that have been game changers.   Your children are watching and listening for your leadership in showing them what THRIVING can mean for all of you.

You got this!

And it's ok to ask for what you need

PARENTS LEADING AND REPAIRING

The first leaders you were ever exposed to were your parents. They taught you how to communicate, influence and/or control others. You learned communication styles, punishment tactics and coping strategies from them. Most likely, you either adopted those teachings or attempted to rebel and do things differently.

When you're under stress, you may revert to your least preferred behaviors. You might catch yourself saying things to your children or your employees that you swore you'd never say. I call this the "dark side" of unconscious patterns that can reveal themselves when stress is highest. Amygdala hijacking!

Emotions are energy, and they can move and change quickly. You will have days when you are more reactive than usual, which can cause you to respond in ways that you regret. One of the most important tools a parent or leader can apply is to **repair**.

Repairing: Owning your regrettable reactions and apologizing for them. This is key to building trusting, connected, relationships with your family and teams.

Emotionally intelligent leaders and parents build stronger, more trusting interpersonal relationships when they repair and take ownership of their behaviors.

HUMOR LOST and FOUND

Having humor during challenging times of stress, is critical to our survival and "thrival." But when we feel stressed, it can be the first thing to go out the window! It can be difficult to see the humor in working from home when your kids are also at home.

Just imagine the look on the faces of the world's working parents, when they were told, "You have to work from home, and, oh by the way, your children will also be home 24/7 and your school age children will need to be homeschooled for the next few months.

You have to laugh! It sounds absurd!

You will need to be able to do it all. I mean DO IT ALL. Work, parent and be a teacher too.

WHAT? You've got to be kidding.

AND, the kids can't go to the park to play, or be outside in public places where too many gather.

When I imagined the faces of the world's parents when they realized they'd all need to live/work/teach from home, my laughter quickly turned to a gut felt sense of THIS SUCKS! This is going to be hard! This is going to be so challenging. I can't imagine how we'll get through this.

The brain can't quite grasp new realities when it's first announced. Yet, parents are able to do what they've done every day since they had their first child, **they adapt**.

Adaptability is one of the 5 capacities of Emotionally Intelligent leaders. Being a good parent also includes having the skill to adapt.

And remember, this is an **<u>EXPERIMENT</u>.**

During experiments, you keep in mind what the outcome is that you desire, test things out, if things fail to produce the result you desired, you try one or two things differently until you get the result you hoped for. All the while, noting what you're learning along the way.

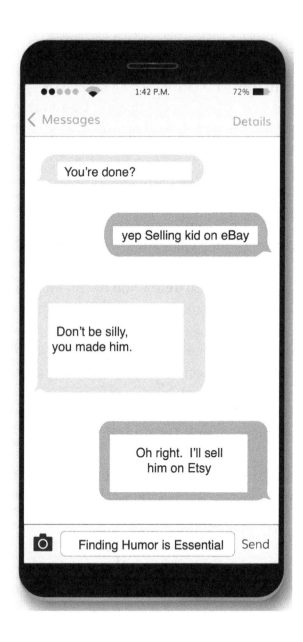

HELPFUL QUOTES to FIND PERSPECTIVE

"One day at a time." - The best advice I've been given from my 91-year-old British Godmother who lived through the war. (In other words, Keep Calm and Carry On!)

"The days are very long, but the years are very short."

"This too shall pass."

"My house looks like I'm losing a game of Jumanji."

"Silence is golden unless you have a toddler, in that case silence is very suspicious and likely dangerous."

"My mom voice was so loud today, my neighbors brushed their teeth and cleaned their rooms."

"After all this parenting I think I'll become a hostage negotiator. Seems less stressful."

"It's day 2 of home schooling and I'm already wondering when teacher appreciation day is."

I'm sure you have your favorites as well.

It's good to laugh daily! Not taking ourselves too seriously is a mighty helpful practice anytime!

BOUNDARIES AND CAPACITY

It's important to monitor and recognize your emotional and intellectual capacity levels when dealing with so many variables and high stressors. When you find your patience running low, it may be time to put some boundaries in place to allow yourself time and space to get back to center.

Boundaries are set to protect you and them. When stress gets too high, you can lose our cool frequently. If you can engage your Intrapersonal self-awareness skills and sense when your tank is empty, you can employ a time-out for yourself and go practice some resilience activities to fill your tank again (see page 18).

One of my coaching clients this past week said, "I have to keep the boundaries of bedtime and quiet time during the day, or else I might just strangle them."

I share this candor (and a sheepish smile) as I personally understand that anyone who has children/teenagers has felt at their wits end as a parent. Our capacity to deal with things fluctuates.

Recognizing the warning signs that your tank is about to be empty is important. These signals can include feeling resentful, irritated or curt. For some you might notice your tone of voice sharpens or experience tension in any part of your body, which could include gut contractions or jaw clenching. You may even experience the desire to run away or flee. We're all human and all these examples are normal.

Our children have capacities that ebb and flow from day to day as well. They learn from **watching** our behaviors, not from what we say.

Teaching our children to recognize when their tanks are empty and helping them to apply resilience practices is one of the best life skills we can teach them. Modeling and incorporating this into your family system is essential for helping create a family that is healthy, centered, and thriving, in challenging times.

Remember that crying is a very effective practice for releasing stress hormones (namely cortisol which can cause cancer, heart disease and other health issues).

Kids and teens also need to have permission to release their emotions to feel relief and get back to center themselves. Note: it can be common for one person in the family feels all the feelings, including those that others, in the family, choose not to feel.

Dr. Aletha Solter, Aware Parenting has authored many books that provide life changing tools to parents. In *Tears and Tantrums* she explains that when children can't cooperate, it's typically a sign they need to release all the stressors accumulated inside. They release somatically through crying or stretching their bodies out, or arching their backs, which helps to release stress hormones and tension. Soma means body.

I grew up in a family where this was not allowed. I chose to follow Dr. Solter's method with my son, and I've experienced the magic of this technique for the past 15 years.

When my son needed to cry or express, I allowed him do so in a safe place (either in my arms or near me). When he was older, he used pillows, sometimes with a small plastic or foam bat.

The body has to express the pent-up emotions or it builds up and prevents sleep, concentration, cooperation, etc. It's a life-saving parenting tool that I highly recommend.

It requires capacity for parents to witness and hold the space for kids to release. If you can master it, though, I guarantee that the outcomes are amazing.

Another sign of emotional intelligence is being comfortable with others' emotions.

Our tears help release stress hormones, therefore crying is healthy for us all.

You've heard of the broken cookie syndrome? When we hold a boundary and say no to our children, this can "trigger" the need-to-unwind stress release or the cookie breaks and they cry. Emotional releases are part of every human experience, just like amygdala hijackings. It's a natural healing process to release.

Giving yourself permission to cry and feel the full range of emotions will increase your capacity to hold your children in their wholeness and resilience too.

In addition to crying, I teach people to **empty out** through writing. I call this learning to "Drop It."

With kids or teens, you can have them write out what's bothering them, and then have them crumple or tear it up and toss it in a fire place or trash. In some cultures, people bury the things that they want to let go of.

Other ways families move energy, soothe and re-center:

- Turn up music and have a dance party
- March with instruments around the house (pots and pans, spoons work too).
- Sing songs, put on shows for each other
- Have pillow fights (rule: no hitting above the neck for safety)
- Bake and cook together
- Craft, complete a project play games together

- Camp or picnic in the back yard or inside
- Read and snuggle together
- Take Vitamin V and Vitamin G (share what you're proud of and what you're grateful for)
- Turn off devices and sleep well – bed by 10 p.m.

Parenting is the hardest job in the world. Have compassion for yourself and for your kids. You're all doing the best you can.

There are more creative resources for you and your family at GrowingUpWhole.com. Guidebooks and validation journals for children, teens and parents. Creative pages filled with fun activities and practices to increase emotional intelligence, health, gratitude, self-esteem, resilience, compassion, naming emotions, communication, finding their passions and wholeness.

Growing Up Whole
A Child's Guide Book   Linda Newlin

BEYOND 2020

Organizations Taking Inspired Action

What will history write
about you and your leaders?

We have never seen in our lifetime this type of global upheaval and risk to personal safety, health, welfare and financial stability for so many.

Companies are scrambling to establish financial mitigation plans and alternative production/product management solutions, in addition to managing nearly a billion people now working from home unexpectedly.

Some organizations have been building their knowledge and capacity to deal with VUCA (Volatility, Uncertainty, Complexity and Ambiguity).

This unforeseen global event has caused immense upheaval, worldwide. **It is VUCA on steroids.**

The markets are volatile and the future is uncertain, and our plan to move forward will be complex and ambiguous. Nothing like this has ever been navigated before.

This is a unique time in every organization's biography to discover their greatest resilience, ingenuity, creativity and resourcefulness. Leaders will likely face some of the toughest decisions and choices of their lives.

There isn't time to analyze why no one saw this coming, or why governments didn't react more responsibly.

Companies around the globe are in a type of war zone. Decisions can literally mean life or death for employees and loved ones regarding exposure to this deadly virus. Leaders are called upon to manage teams working from home, and enacting immediate safety measures for those still required to work with the public.

There are shortages of materials, supply chains are disrupted and industries are experiencing complete shut downs.

The organizations who will thrive are those who will be able to engage everyone's ability to be creative, resourceful and break out of mindsets and beliefs that no longer apply.

Those who thrive may well shed the brick and mortar mentality to explore and reconfigure the ideal way to work, grow and prosper.

What will you and your leaders do to keep the company alive, shift into new markets, and protect your employees financially and physically?

It's been in great crises that the world's best leaders have emerged. History will take note of those who rise to lead companies in 2020 and beyond with:

> Powerful Persistence
>
> Brave Determination
>
> Bold Courage
>
> Humble Sacrifice
>
> Creative Innovation
>
> Collaboration
>
> Inquisitiveness
>
> Imagination
>
> Curiosity
>
> Compassion

We are seeing great leadership already emerging and it's inspiring. Financial institutions are implementing hardship programs for their customers.

CEO's and senior executives are taking pay cuts to save their employee's jobs.

Health care HEROES are risking their lives every day on the front lines. Thank you from all of us!

These are inspired actions, indeed.

Will your company shift and thrive?

I hope there will be hundreds of inspiring stories to share in the years ahead and I look forward to writing about the heroes in your company and your community, who model the best of humanity and leadership in our future world.

I wish you great strength, health and inspired action to do what is yours to do now and beyond 2020.

Thrive on!

Linda

~~~~~~

"In the silence we can hear what wants to happen next."

Rick Snyder, Author of Decisive Intuition

Other Books by Author Linda Newlin

Drop It: A Coach's Secret to Productivity, Presence and Possibility

Growing Up Whole: A Child's Guide Book

Being Whole: A Teen's Guide Book

Living Whole: A Guide Book for Adults

Validation Journals are available for each of these guidebooks in the series for each age group.

http://growingupwhole.com/ has free songs to enjoy!

The Inner Traveler's GuideBook to Moyo: Discovering the Power of Listening to Your Own Heart

All books are available on Amazon.com

New Fast Read Books that will be released in 2020:

GirlsDads: Raising Daughters Up Right
   Be part of our research – go to website www.GirlDadsBook.com

Drop It 2.0: A program to increase focus & efficiency

Linda Newlin, is a Master Certified Coach, Leadership expert, Author, Speaker, HR Strategic Partner, Search Consultant and Work from Home expert who has provided executive coaching, leadership development and global change management for the past 30 years. She was the pioneer in on-boarding in 1990 when she founded her unique search firm. She has worked with over 2500 leaders globally within: 3M, Microsoft, PWC, Booz Allen, Merrill Lynch, T. Rowe Price, Deutsche Banc, PacifiCare Health Systems, KaVoKerr, Genentech, Starbucks and Harvard.

Linda worked for the American Express Co. in Human Resources and at Pepperdine University's Presidential Key Executive MBA school early in her career.

Linda co-created the *Inner Work of Leaders* course while on faculty at the Hoffman Institute. Her passion for creating sustainable change and life enhancing practices are reflected in her many books and music that she writes: 2BWhole.com highlights her book series for children, teens and adults which teach critical life skills around health, non-violent communication, boundary setting, self-love and self-esteem, environmental stewardship, naming emotions, visioning, resilience and validation.

Linda is active in many organizations and non-profits and was awarded the ***Everyday Hero Award*** by the Up With People Alumni Association for her on-going work to support children and adults to gain valuable life skills and resilience after trauma. She gives a portion of all her books to organizations who support women in transition and leaders who can impact positive change globally.

Books, eLearning & Virtual Coaching Resources

What Got You Here, Won't Get You There by Marshall Goldsmith

Take The Lead by Betsy Myers

Coach Your Self Up by Mike Normant

Decisive Intuition by Rick Snyder

Humane Leadership by Stephen Sloan

Stress Less, Accomplish More by Emily Fletcher

Tears and Tantrums, Raising Drug Free Kids, The Aware Baby, by Dr. Aletha Solter

Conscious Leadership & Creating High Performing Teams by Rebecca Watson

Inner Professional eLearning Catalog

Coach Your Self Up Course

Emotions at Work

Mindful at Work

These and more at www.Innerplicity.com

Virtual coaching for individuals and teams

Intuition University Sales, Innovation, Leadership